Ferndown Library
Tel: 01202 674542

FDANF

GW00499849

- Please return items before closing time
  on the last date stamped to avoid charges.
- Renew books by phoning 01305 224311 or
  online www.dorsetforyou.com/libraries
- Items may be returned to any Dorset library.
- Please note that children's books issued on
  an adult card will incur overdue charges.

Dorset County Council
Library Service

DL/2372 dd05450

Gallery Books
Editor Peter Fallon

X

Vona Groarke

Gallery Books

X
is first published
simultaneously in paperback
and in a clothbound edition
on 27 February 2014.

The Gallery Press
Loughcrew
Oldcastle
County Meath
Ireland

www.gallerypress.com

ISBN 978 1 85235 576 0 *paperback*
     978 1 85235 577 7 *clothbound*

A CIP catalogue record for this book
is available from the British Library.

Contents

René Descartes' La Géométrie (1637) introduces the use of the first letters of the alphabet to signify known *quantities and the use of the last letters to signify* unknown *quantities.*
— Florian Cajori, *A History of Mathematical Notations*
(Chicago, 1928)

A Pocket Mirror

The day the first snowdrop in my winter garden insists
in its own insistent way that the promise I buried
last September would finally come to light, I wake
to the hoops the woodpigeon puts himself through.
Either that or to bells, bells on a loop, going over
and over the selfsame crucial news as yesterday.

What is it I keep this tentative record of? For what reason
do I step along high words with immeasurable care
or list the fanciful logic of one moment, then another?
Is it to do with allegiance, perhaps, with how a snowdrop
keeps faith with the world, or a pocket mirror,
matt on one side, is true to life on the other?

The White Year

I am told that memory can't afford
to care less about what it brings to light
just as I'm told the table does not

occupy itself with cleanliness
nor the made bed with desire,
but it is difficult to believe.

I do not imagine it simple to strip
from any given afternoon
the intentions of the day.

Not when a contingent darkness
announces itself at the door
like an ordinary to-do

and not when, in the winter garden,
the beautifully managed trees
toy with shadows of themselves.

A skim of plausible survival
settles on what I do while, in the museum
of the everyday, no dust whatsoever

is to be found on the bedside chair,
unopened perfume,
impeccable gold quilt.

It may well be possible to separate
into a fiction of forgetfulness,
the accomplished house,

but I don't believe in it either.
There is before and after,
surely, and there is discretion

to be accounted for, and grief,
night after night, city after city,
word after functional word.

This is whatever time I have.
My whole body has to find a way
to be in possession of itself

like a shop selling only white things
or the way two bridges on the same river
will have knowledge of each other.

X

straight lines only
no curve or arc
to double back

no circle in sight
from which silence might slip
like the strap of a dress
off a shoulder
one summer field

a shape
signifying nothing
but a puzzle of itself
made in the box of morning
untangled over years

from each and every corner of which
is visible white space
as if here and now
were equal lines
fused the way lovers are fused
for as long as it takes
to pass through the eye of love
to recover, to egress.

Brushstroked husband
and brushstroked wife
finding in skewered union
a defence of loneliness

sectioning in four equal parts,
as if it were a family,
that safe place,

once being
full of itself,
now cornered, quartered, hinged

on a mark that closes
on common darkness
the heart of which is silence, certainly,
a need expressed in what distends
beyond what will not be
acknowledged,
what will not be
allowed

the length and breadth of days
that bleed into other days
on which occurs
an ardent solitude —

windows opening and closing the one sky.

I may begin to fold myself
along four even lines
into the centre of those days

to learn how a life may come to rest
on the absence of a life

as crosshairs train on a blank page

as arrows turn in on themselves

as the blades of a bedroom ceiling fan
come to

a perfectly obvious stop.

Aubade

That was yesterday. Innumerable blues seeped away into a night of shadow where shadow ought to be. They spun it out, fingers strumming the gloss of another evening on my own. I thought it would be more: something to pass, as church bells do, for love. My words gave out: they couldn't stand that depth of optimism. They have acquired holes through which the sense of what I mean slips in. I could say I am lonesome and the words would laugh their tin laugh back at me. I could say I am venturesome beyond a wish to stopper up a ticking wound with consonants and vowels. I could write myself out of the marl pit, line by line. I do my best to pay attention to the shifting of the mechanism that delivers me, first light, to my found self. The morning headlongs through lives I know nothing about, to come full stop on the pillow beside mine. When I turn the image over, it rattles like a blown bulb in which slight words foresee straightforward ends. Every hour slots into a previous hour's slot. The ratio of memory to loss upends itself. I do not see why it should be necessary to go over and over it, but there is a length of bright orange silk. And it is by my hand.

Where She Imagines the Want of Being Alone

A small house. Rooms with white door handles
and a dangerous sky to be trapped in window frames.

It is, she thinks, a house for clear glass bowls
and slight intentions. She writes she hears, early nights,

ordinary disappointments rattle, single grains
of rice in a jar, one box inside another.

Something in her wishes to acknowledge
the nothing she has known of love,

but this cannot be the house for that
with its too much time.

3

It is late. The night is required to fold itself up
into squares that get smaller and smaller
the more I notice them. I am learning
to pay attention to this narrow, straight-line house
that must have had all its corners by heart before
ever I came to fit my life snug under its eaves.

I could count the balustrade shadows as standing in
for decades, or for owners, in my stead, and know
it is not for me to believe they left nothing behind:
nothing in how a door will open or a door will close,
or a window lean into what the rowan tree has to say.
The banister's way with three hinged centuries
has more heat in it than it needs to have, even on this
July evening when the rooms at the top of the house
vouchsafe another summer day tomorrow.

I am the clean slate. I am off-white walls
and open windows, a garden planted from scratch.
I am floor-length curtains and bookcases,
rooms that listen nicely to each other.
I am door knobs and reading lamps, blue glass
bowls on window sills, family photographs,
corners with silence in them, that sly peace,
a contrivance to which my blue and white hours
and too much clean bed linen give the lie.

My house of uneven numbers,
of my children's hyphenated lives.
My house of small hours, of voices
a little quieter than they need to be.
Our summer is all in paragraphs,
everything supposedly given to light,
despite the slip in every corner
with a May date written on it

by ghosts who listen to everything,
but cannot make sense of it; who gather
in their arms what light the house holds,
pooling it in doorways so none of us
will ever have to step out into dark;
who fret the dog every now and then and,
to make up for it, ruffle lavender in its pots
so the scent slips in the back door; who play
noughts and crosses in the trellis shadow
and don't care who loses, who wins.

The Storm

The storm presents itself
on the stage of my window
with too much show

to be on terms with its backdrop
and yet it has to be
reckoned with

though it be dressed to the nines
in costume jewellery
and colours that don't go.

It is like lines with too much hope
that want to be made allowance for
and still want to be true.

I am not ashamed
of anything in my life,
but there is the business

of a price to be paid
for the want of love,
how it is beyond me

that I would press
an ordinary storm
to intimate metaphor,

so the mime of lightning
and the mimicry of thunder
would silence between them

the photograph of not-me
in a summer field, and no sign
of the taking hand

when I really should be
listening, I know,
with my eyes shut fast

to learn what might
steady me: the music
of a stone in rain

or a swan in darkness
down by the docks
making shelter of itself

or a tin roof talking back
to weather in a night
unspoken for.

Fate

I do not know what it is in me
that would want to bunker down

in a fairy story that could nutshell
nine hundred years to my two

and would have me speak
with the throat of a bird

or the throat of a reed
by the side of a lake

with nowhere to go.

That would have me exchange
my blue and white bedroom for feathers,

cups of gold for handfuls of sand,
love for thunder and brine.

Except this. I toy with banishment
a second time and a third

but my heart isn't in it.
I already know

that if I have been required to fly
over the history of my house

and see only nettles and scutch
where my children's home should be,

then I will also be woken by bells
with their eight o'clock definite truth

so I may walk in the room
of my own breath

and say we will leave it at that.

Furrow

Though scooped with my printed fingers
and lined with remnants of ink

the furrow's trench-like depression
knows nothing, or almost nothing,

of the barrow's burial mound. Pages flutter
between them, ornamentally,

and it is only a matter of sound
before elision, or collapse.

Into which, complicitly,
I would ease myself,

for what I'm not allowed say,
but to lay down my head in furlough nouns

that have shed every memory of you.
But there I will not lie again.

There is at stake an honesty
in knowing, definitively, what is meant

by walking into a moment
and taking the measure of it,

of what the first hand might have to declare
if the second weren't so loud,

of how they occupy each other,
to arrive at a single end.

How little I comprehend any of this,
the faithless slippage of things.

How years, like words, silt up in themselves:
how, when I'm taking the bus home,

I'm also hitchhiking to years ago
to fill in both our names on a form

or am sitting at a yellow table
in a restaurant called *Now*.

You have come on foot to visit
and I am waiting for you.

The Galway Train

From it, it's possible, possibly,
to translate a shadow's down payment
on the side of a hill

to a blatant future where one could admit
'I was in love' or 'I was younger then'
to be nothing more or less credible than

the throb of ragwort, excitable windows,
a sincere line of rowans by the road.

A field's intake of breath
could be the thing.

I think that what I make of it
is rampant privacy,

a way of extending
what I see to be true
past this specific urgency,

this journey slipping out, like twine,
of a knot that does not take

to, for a finish,
the kind of promise
a field of buttercups
can make.

Equinox

Being known for miles around by hilltop trees
and a way with the rising or the setting sun,
everything dark within for the rest of the year
becoming a matter of light, a space disclosed
for just this once (calling Antony Gormley's
orifice etchings in 'Body and Soul' to mind).

Hitching back roads to the passage tomb, never
arriving there. Wanting to settle in us being us,
wishing there be an incremental scale, a measure
of brightness, showing up every progress between
us, shucking off every one black minute, turning
ourselves, our very selves, shamelessly, inside out.

'La Route'

— André Derain (1932)

Three bars of shadow on a yellow road,
a sky of Chinese blue.
Though there is only the road
and its sidelong songs
to mark time with you, walk on.
Trees talking shadow talk
will make no mention of you.

With your ashplant and knapsack,
you have no notion of rain
or thunder with no rain in it
scarcely worth sheltering from,
even if the village had roofs
and doors to the houses,
music to its two streets.

If you are sorry, as I was,
that you didn't bring bread with you
and something to wash it down
and maybe a fig for afterwards,
don't give it another thought.
This is one of many villages
that turns its open palms up to the sun.

Next along the yellow road
another town will occur to you,
this time approached by a bridge.
You will hear cowbells and church bells
and a donkey whingeing at them.

You will smell loaves rising
and you will quicken your step
until your footprints in the dust

fall upon footprints in the dust
to lead you to a stranger's door.

No one will be surprised to see you
for your own two children
will be waiting there
with a welcome for you
like a jar of wildflowers
and no harm done.

Is It Time?

The children will be waiting for me
with blue-veined arms and all tomorrow
slaked in the whites of their eyes.

They have knowledge, they assure me,
of how rain comes undone
and mornings thicken like milk.

They remember the story of the night
that popped itself inside out
and forgot all of its songs.

'But what happened the moon?'
Picked up, shiny penny, by a woman
with too much air in her pockets,

spent on a word from a barrow seller
and gifted, in turn, to a boy and a girl
who learn what becomes of it.

The Box

I sat in a garden of medieval wildflowers
and let the sun insist upon my face.
There was a city at my back
with the kind of light at play

that had knowledge of blue enamel
and chinoiserie,
limestone carved into a sleeve,
the river's secular motet.

I was thinking of the silver box
I hadn't bought at the market stall,

of how I might have opened it
there in the tapestry garden,
let the dust of all that feeling,
all those words, fall at my feet.

It was June and the two years were up.
I had no sense to make of it.
The city passed its small gold coins
from one hand to the other.

The Wrong Silence

These are the hours that cannot be reasoned with,
when a black wind pours through the islands
into the throat of the bay.

When the morning hears the wrong silence,
the afternoon practices too many lies
and the evening believes them.

There is talk of a purple box
washed up on the rocks
in which are written

names of wildflowers
and names of winds
and a name for what's yet to be loved.

When All This Is Done, Sure

If I liken you to anything
it will probably have to be

the small boy on the A-train
with a xylophone on his lap.

When the doors close
nothing is left of him

but precise, metallic silence
where his four right notes have been.

Just Exactly That Kind of Day

A summer Saturday pitched
like a mansard roof made of red tiles,
leftover minutes from the week just gone,
squares of music rehearsing a fall
as ticker tape from open windows
any street you care to cross.

In such a come day, go day kind of town,
I wonder what fractional slippage of love
might think itself so obvious as this.

And the wondering is like
when something's lost
and you look everywhere
but it's not to be found
until there it is
right in front of your eyes

and still you keep on looking.

The Front Door

The sky inside my head grows out
of a single cell of blue. One minute,
I'm snicking geraniums and, before you know it,
there's larks and curlews and a jet-trail
with no beginning to it unzipping my last thought.

One minute, I'm pinning my to-do list,
like a discouraged orchid, to the day;
the next, here in the kitchen,
the night's two plums are bedding down
in their black lacquer bowl.

Between, the day rises to a skim of meaning,
the bright blue door opening into what
I think I know. Everything else is an eye
of daylight through which is streaming,
time and again, what all happens next.

Midsummer

All to play for. Yesterday the rain kept hinting
it had something else to say. Today is a garden
with clothes on the line that smell of childhood
and the kind of endings that fold themselves
into tidy squares within arm's reach of the sea.
Today is tilted skylights and doors held open
with bricks. Today is next door breaking eggs
on the edge of a glass bowl. Today is a phrase
learned off by heart by asters and peonies. Also,
by fuchsia and mallow. And everything between.

Tonight I will sleep on a sheet that had joy
of a barefaced sun above the cherry tree
and tonight there will be two hundred moons
stowed between panes of double glazing
in both my dovetailed dreams of being here.

Going Out

for Eve

My daughter, heading out on the town in her glad rags,
laughs a laugh like a floribunda rose pinned in her hair.
She has so much beauty in her, more than this summer
evening, in all its frippery. More, even, than the sound
of her heels the length of the road, her phone voice
dipping into company, the pooled high talk of her
and her friends slipping through the city's open door.

Do me a favour, daughter: sometime, in time, wear for me
a sweetheart neckline, slingback sandals, my good ring
and howsoever many of your necklaces and bracelets.
Walk your walk through ten thousand doorways
so the music of you is one and the same as the music
of starlings and new moons and traffic lights and weirs,
only in a new arrangement arranged by, and for, you.

Lessons of the Garden

1

The trick is to lift clean off the sea
     its one scarce stain
and transplant it to my satisfactory garden
     that needs to learn
the ins and outs of how the colour blue
     can read itself
like a story that closes unfathomably
     or a word
with a silent ending, shadow-blind.

2

It should be easy to say
the garden speaks
with the silver of wood
left out over winter
in all weathers.

But it is not.

Not when the garden speaks
a speech that has a lost brooch in it,
a brooch with weeping willows
set in pearls, dropped between rocks
fetched up by my hand
and set down in this soil
to be overheard every day
promising a clean alone
first thing.

3

My garden regards me as a lover might
across a room of business and words
to a silence full of itself.

Here is all my new beginning.
Here is the wild love seeded in me
I hoped would get to air before nightfall.

4

A garden intimate with all its lies
will practise surface gestures of release
the way water will, but holding something back.

Oh, where is the wave that broke on his skin
and where is the sunlight to earth it?

I turn this over, nightly, between thumbs.

5

The wood pigeon's carry-on in the rowan
and what a cloth on the line has to say

the claim staked by roots in the wildflower patch
and the fuchsia's history of home

the air in the back-door keyhole
and words taking shape in my mouth

amount to the same thing
and what the same thing reasons is

Let go.

6

There is one moon lodged in the cherry tree
and another, simpler, one above the rowan.

My bed is a small boat determined to sail
between hazard and current, weather and sway.

I close the window, re-set the sky, pull the room
around my shoulders, count the moon.

The Garden Sequence

THE GARDEN AS MUSIC AND SILENCE

Only a roofline tin whistle
practising 'The Parting Glass'
construes the gap
between lupin and rose
as possible held breath.

Inside of which
it falls to me to imagine
the blue of cornflowers
has knowledge
of gothic windows
and tapestried plainsong.

Also, that Tuesday's red geraniums
might have something to say
about avowal

and the poppy seedheads
something about
presentiment

they learn
to keep
to themselves.

THE GARDEN IN HINDSIGHT

Those black tulips that never put forth
so much as a single bloom,

would they be as close in themselves
this day as the day we upped sticks

to three houses ago, our belongings
in numbered boxes, seven years

as a handful of soil in a page
between me and my winter coat?

Tonight, as the year hoists itself north,
I imagine them still there, winter

by winter, learning to turn embittered
hearts against all possible sky

and every tulip planted since
a righting of the weight of darkness

pressed by my hand to lodge and yield
as to remembered light.

THE GARDEN IN SENTIMENT

Because she picked for him
one bud of Albertine rose,

laced it through his work-suit lapel
and straight-pinned the stem behind;

because he watched her do it,
kissed her forehead,

then kissed her hand;
and because I watched them

from the first of summer,
one June, lives ago,

I keep no Albertine in my garden.
There is no need for it.

THE WHITE GARDEN

The foolish moon
unhinged by darkness
has a word

for the white poppy
and the table top
of Carrara marble

set with tea from China
and cups from a town
surrounded by hills.

Come the rain,
the candy-stripe
of the summer chair

will muster a circus
on my watch
and drips from the gutter

march a marching band
from one fence
to the other.

Come the wind,
the garden will hold up
two clenched fists

and shout a hundred answers
to questions I
have not asked

and afterwards
will have me to know
the promise of

one kind of love
never leaning
against any other.

Come morning, the bud vase
with the yellow flower
will do as best it can

but what colour
is the colour of where
the last moon used to be?

THE GARDEN AS EVENT

The briars are twined to the fencing post
and the afternoon staked to two kinds of hour,
the narrow, answered by coffee cups
or birdsong run amok,

the other, stretched to the edge of the city
like the skin of a drum on which
someone is keeping time, bald time,
with a persistent heart.

I could drop a question on its surface
and it would bounce, slight answer
to what the skyline asks of the sky;
the branch, of the cherry tree.

In the milk-white kitchen
nothing has changed for an hour
or more: the lettuce is upright
in the window trough

and the cut-glass vase on the table top
has nothing to add to the square of light
slipping off a neighbour's patio door
one street to the back.

Knives whittle patience in the drawer
and fruit in the fruit bowl glosses
a composed version of itself.
The front door holds its breath.

All this happens, is happening
without me, in much the same way

as the cowslips make sense
of their borrowed pot

or winter slumps in the green bin
or shallow leaves fathom
the azalea I earthed
and the rowan I did not.

THE SIX GARDENS OF METAPHOR

for Tommy

One is a wood of a single tree
    a branch with metal leaves attached
    by way of a copper beech.

One is a river
    a length of brown ribbon tied to
    a needle of pure gold.

One is an ocean
    sea-heath and sea-holly
    with an undertow of moss.

One is a mountain
    a stretch of centuries
    within a pebble's reach.

One is mist in a hollow
    an acer over gravel
    raked to a new day.

One is the future
    readied for you
    behind this bamboo screen.

THE BLUE GARDEN

Bluebell or cornflower, it's all the one
to the cherry tree with its many doors
opening, hour by hour, on one colour
as rooms with forgetful walls might do,
their layers of paint and antique paper
golden with birds and golden flowers,
hunkering under a whim of novelty.

By such means does the day
take the trouble to explain
how the blackbird in the cherry tree
makes it his business to assemble
in its simple branches a home
one takes for an inside world
crowded with golden songs.

By such means do I slip myself
into the ink of assembled flowers,
lavender and forget-me-not,
sea-holly and allium all the one
to the cherry tree, its papery blossom
and the blackbird in my sky-blue study
making bits of song out of his day.

THE GARDEN AS AN ISLAND APPROACHED
BY A TIDAL CAUSEWAY

Whole stretches when the stretch between
the bottom step and the raised beds
becomes impassable.

Only just now
I walked to the white rose
to pay my compliments

and now already I can barely
make it out, so far-fetched
is the water in between.

It has unpicked the geometry
of limestone slabs, smoothing
socket and furrow, evening itself.

It sucks at the struts of the wooden steps
where I stand in my bare feet,
my mouth dry, my hand empty.

A word passes from one to the other.
I know this word, how it falls
the way the past falls,

splinters under me.
I also know how soil
behind sleepers

will eventually rise to it
and all my scheme and wager
come undone.

Who can say,
as the timetable does,
exactly when, to the very minute,

the garden will prove itself
so that I may step
from this last step

out of hinterland
and aftermath
onto emergent ground?

THE GARDEN, FROM ABOVE

Like catching sight of a sleeping body
from an open bedroom door,
and staying because you know this body
has no one to watch over it
in the usual run of things

and wanting to watch, to lightly watch,
if only for a minute, if only to stake
whatever it is that is staked
by one body in sight of another
and no love between

but something beyond love:
vigilance, maybe, or kindness
though no kindness is offered
and no kindness received.
Something like a name

let slip from an upstairs window
into a slipstream of summer,
let to sway like grass in heat
and come asunder even
before it comes to rest

on the thorn of a tea rose
or on the petal of rust
that falls from the hinge
of the window it falls from
as your breath becomes

the air you breathe; your gaze
a frame of its own devising

within which the garden settles,
turns in on itself,
leaves you to turn away.

THE GARDEN AS A GARDEN

Cornflower pods may split to yield
a summer evening or a yellow blouse
but the garden remains every garden
I ever thought to make,

the trellis threaded
by an Albertine I carried
with me through four decades
in a sky-blue pot.

Mine for summer. Mine for the year.
Mindful that what the garden cherishes
is the lapse between sun-up
and the first glance thrown its way

when it gathers itself,
calms the earthen ache in its bones
and embroiders on its blue-veined skin
whatever day will come,

flower by flower
inveigled out of those blue years
to the point of where I am
or the point where I am not.

Oh, garden strung between
cherry and rowan, absolve
each trace of my desiring,
remember nothing of me.

THE GARDEN IN WINTER

Against the orange of rowan berries,
debutante hollyhocks turn dowdy
and nasturtiums seem old hat.
I make an hour's work out of spilling
cornflower seedpods out into air
without a hint of blue in it all summer.
My antic husbandry. I let the gooseberries
rot for not knowing when to pick them
and tied sweet peas to driftwood stakes
with too much ocean still in them. Soon,
it will be time to bring geraniums indoors,
marshal them under the console table
to sit out weather people fret about.
Already, nights have a seam of frost
in which the stitching is coming loose.
Dark hours rummage through the rooms
so my heart (that dogged, little thing)
learns to accept itself as autumnal
in a plangent, bulb-lit sort of way.
No telling when one thought
becomes another;
when the very idea
of the garden in winter
slips into the notion
that life, on its own,
is not nearly enough.

THE NEW GARDEN

for Helen O'Leary

In our inland gardens the sea
with its freight of sorrowful songs
becomes a question answered by years
and poppies with their grown children,
their sunspilt photographs.

A light blue door with butterfly hinges
and a seedhead lock is opening for us.
And here we are in what we do
courtesy of unphased colour
pinned to sentences and air,

straight lines with the past in them
and something else besides
to put as we wish in ungilded frames
one white rose after another
until the garden is done with summer,

yes, our loss. No way back but back again
to gardens that forget themselves
for whole months at a time
only to turn out their box of tricks
at the first tilt of new light.

THE GARDEN, OVER TIME

Mine for now, a smallholding
with time on its hands
and a way of shuffling months
as if they were tarot cards,

come good
for the most part
better than desiring
had foretold.

Even the hole where
the wrong maple
scarce one month in
closed over that false start:

though seeming
as if everything bad
I knew of the world
was lodged in that absence

it passed, just as
summer's ardour
was put to rights
by months of rigour

and withdrawal, like
small hours to be
thrown ahead,
picked up down

the day. I replaced
the maple with

a mannerly box,
put down forty, fifty bulbs

to gainsay a new year.
Meanwhile,
the bones of winter
harvested

like fallen twigs
and knocked together,
once, for luck,
ring hollow as words

I would just as soon
shroud in darkness
as bring to
open light:

how much longer
until I am planted,
bulb in winter,
in my parents' soil?

October the last.
Summer hands me
its box of colour
to stow

with the Sweet Afton tin
of silk embroidery thread.
Is it, they ask each other,
just a question

of clairvoyance,
of drawing the line

between what's known
and what's to come,

of hearing, the way
a blackbird does
the invisible worm,
what darkness makes of itself?

I may bring to fruition
predictions
I hardly bother to make
this side of things

or I may not.
The stained glass mobiles
on the patio
think it is summer;

fine by me.
It seems like no time
no time at all
has melted on my tongue

since I first hung them
against light. Left
to my alone devices,
I would spend it, surely,

cradling the only
fact of winter
coming in early,
yes, this year.

The White Boat

The boat that sailed across scorched earth
is white and has a painted sail
and is not the same boat
yet found abandoned
at the bottom of the well.

No. The boat that sailed across scorched earth
was made of mica and feathers
and coated in a lacquer of infinite loneliness.

The boat that sailed across scorched earth
was put together in a mirrored workshop
that knew only stalwart skies.

No one is allowed to sail in her
least of all by me.

Effet de Crépuscule

An inlet with a bay at the back of its mind puts you in mind
of Cuisin's crepuscular waterways, how they seeped, it's said,
into Chopin's nocturnes, lines of branches and towpaths
and railings as nothing compared with the pleated notes
in which darkness folds and unfolds itself along a seam
of midnight or an edging of backlit cloud. West again,
done with the day, you take the coast road, its tentative bridge
over an away tide. There is a hill you will climb to your B&B
and a sequence of dreams like rented rooms where nothing
is yours but a second-hand suitcase you barely recognize.
You turn. A navy slip of September dusk is pulled down
over upstretched trees and chimneys and telegraph poles.
The town might as well hold its breath the way the inlet does
for the alone woman by a painted tree, barely visible save
for a white scarf, waiting by a barque that is waiting for her
to step with all her unverbed ghosts out into final light.

The Ghost on the Road

He comes only in rain,
walks out of the bend to call on me,
composed as a sapling.

He looks up at my window,
just the once

but I know that look
and everything that will come of it
given ink and time.

The ghost on the road walks
his every step into my breath.

His hands, I remember,
make a drum of my skin
that years fall on

and the sound of them,
darker than it was,

is the grey of a road
with no one on it.

The ghost on the road
takes his time
in getting to my gate.

He has as long as rain
and so do I.

With his woodcutter's scar
and the smoke in his throat;

with his clasp of islands
and his orchid mind

I see in him these words.

His love is the weight of every time
he has come this way before

but I am a shadow behind glass

and the ghost on the road
is a ghost on the road

for all I make of him.

Ghost Poem

Crowded at my window tonight, your ghosts
will have nothing to speak of but love
though the long grass leading to my door
is parted neither by you, leaving

nor by you, coming here. The same ghosts
keep in with my blood, the way
a small name says itself, over
and over, so one minute is cavernous

compared to the next, and I cannot locate
words enough to tell you your wrist
on my breast had the same two sounds to it.
You are a sky over narrow water

and the ghosts at my window
are a full day until I shed their loss.
I want to tell you all their bone-white,
straight-line prophecies

but the thought of you, this and every night,
is your veins in silverpoint mapped
on my skin, your life on mine
that I made up and lived inside, as real,

and I find I cannot speak of love
or any of its wind-torn ghosts to you
who promised warm sheets and a candle, lit,
but promised me in words.

The Road

There is a road a child could draw
with charcoal or black crayon
from one edge to another
of a sheet of white.

Any child could manage it:
it does not have to be a happy child.

That is a road I would find myself on,
if only as a stone in the middle,
the way love is: correct, plausible,
willful; awfully sure of itself.

The Featherstore, St Kilda

Not hail on your slates. Not caulk
coming loose from a ruin of a gable wall.

Not words with a stone at the centre.
Not a remnant of winter.

Not a memory rolling downslope
upon your ghosted sleep.

Let it be feathers, do.
A vigil of them. A shimmer. A swoon.

Let my every second thought of you
slip up between your light of day

and my own, an hour lesser, less.
This south of you, our conjoined silences'

soft fall falls as no fair estimate
of what's between us. And the rest of it.

Aubade, Winter Solstice

1

The sun sidles left to right
like a small child
not yet learned to walk,
along rooftops
one road over.

Scarcely one full silence
until it fulfils itself
in the window frame
and accedes
to a meaningless sky.

My midland mind,
all flats and rim, and barely
a hill or a hillside there
to prophesy tomorrow
struggles likewise with uprise.

It wants to believe
that a curious sun will turn
its misgiven questions
on their heads,
but by eleven

nothing has changed
except that morning
has yet to release
each and every promise
from my white bed.

Where I would take you
given the chance,
ask you to quote

the first ripe hour
between us.

My nine o'clock lover,
let your mouth be
the small of winter,
my tongue one word
for light.

2

This morning I call up
sun through muslin
filling our names

so all our senses
are fine, gold wire
unspooling in our hands

and branches tip an only blue
in much the way
your eyelashes do, my breast

or your back is a scoop of decades
linked by chorus
and roofline.

The sky is the soft
of flesh of an hour
we skin with our teeth

and let to fill the rift between
the rise of your mouth
and my own.

Seven times I listen to
the knot of you come undone
the last one being

upon your tongue
a word no one has spoken
or has any meaning for.

High Notes

On a train threading the eye of north
it is nothing to begin to collapse
the various silence the city required of me:
to find in the high notes of the brakes
the scarlet lining of a dark coat
or the single lit office on a top floor;
to listen for the shape of a name
through glass at a station stop;
to observe the fields of an afternoon,
the way they chase each other down
in the kind of blue that learned abstraction
moons ago, how they resolve themselves
into a love poem for no one in particular,
written to be open, for the sake of openness,
this night and every budding night inside.

Closing Time

What you take for company
when the moon is in the rowan
and winter scratches the back door
is the offhand innocence
that would trim any given story
to suit the music of a gate
with raindrops on it
or a street breathing
through a keyhole
or a page turning in darkness
as if it had something to say.

Music from Home

Six inches of weather, New Year's Eve.
I drain a tumbler of homespun
and plump up sentiment
like a goose-down pillow.

The blue flame of the gas fire
sputters its notion of frost
as we count down
to the time-lag pip
of midnight's cheap champagne.

The lines are down.
The radio warns that secondary roads
are nigh impassable.

Come the tune and the first notes
of the opening year's slow air,
the blue lights of the melodeon stipple
two provinces, a river, slip of sea

and the fiddle in all its finery
leans into silver promises
it cannot hope to keep.

Interval

Between acts, mindful
of the present tense
but beholden to what
has already occurred
or what might be going to

as a noun between two verbs
comes to marrow them both
until there is still enough
for the next thing to happen
and be happening again

in the way the opening note
of the second half
has the last note by heart
but doesn't either recall or predict
what plays out over time.

Better to aspire
to knowing as much
of what's done
and what remains to be done
as the pure note on the violin

knows about purfling
or applause, or about
the mastodon tusk
or Mongolian mare's tail
that goes into making the bow.

One Possible Meaning for Rain

Like stepping out of industrial weather
to a lamplit street's doorway . . .

At your back, a sequence of lives plays out separate rooms.
In front, the rain makes free with empty streets,
and you are in on the emptiness.

On the foyer lift, red numbers brighten and darken again.
Doors open, doors close; nobody steps out.
You think the rain will exhaust itself, make way for you

to re-enter a city where you know no one by name,
where no one can claim a single fact about you,
bar your having been there. You will pick up

your journey, that is all. The city will occur to you
all over again and this moment that is not,
but somewhere time has lost the measure of itself,

be only as significant as noirish rain and teeming lives
that are nothing to do with you, that pronounce themselves
above and beyond any word you care to choose.

Of which you are unaccountably innocent.
You could hold out your open hand, let it fill
with what is happening. But you don't.

The Photograph

The whole arc
of what is happening
extends itself
over the bay
of morning
to let its greens
and oranges
insinuate themselves
out of shadow
where a shadow
ought to be.

But what are we to make
of a slip of unscheduled silver
across the window
on the second floor,
as like as not to be
a smudge, let's say,
of a given hand
as he sets down
a cup and saucer
so he can tend geraniums,
greet his buoyant wife,
or make plans for the day
and step into them
unrendered, unawares

which might be something akin
to the way I see you
in your room of rooms
going through motions
I allow for
maybe because I know how to
or simply because I can.

Architecture

This wall is my everyday friend.
— Le Corbusier

Say what you like
but a five shilling lamp that throws
a hundred dollars at the night
or three nectarines ripening the window sill

may make an offer to a world
that sometimes, I swear,
thinks too much of itself
to accept everything.

Words like stones with sunlight on them
lead me to believe
that if I put what I know into bricks and mortar
and paint the plaster white

or position a square of dark blue glass
underneath a square of red,
I would say as much.

The image predicts another image,
one solid phrase and then another
until there is a wall
to depend on

and then a second wall
at a right angle to the first
and a need, suddenly, for a curve,

hence the skin of a nectarine
or the weathered edge of stone
or a skim of light
in the vertical evening

that takes on board whys and wherefores
but arrives at the same conclusion
as a morning come dressed in lined grey silk
to take us out of ourselves.

How to Read a Building

Don't. You might as well say a morning convenes
in panelled reflections of itself. Or call the way
a roofline predicts its likely outcome, fate. Write 'arch',
so the word has to position itself between noun
and adjective. Put 'Lintel' as a title: see what comes of it.
I, too, may think of line endings with every quoin
or cant; of surface meaning caulked airtight;
of metaphor constructed as a tinted curtain wall.
I am alive, yes, to the notion of cantilevered sound,
open to rhymes between stone and stained glass,
sunlight and cement. Say what you like, there's a name
for every kind of window you could possibly
see through. But the room with no window
has no first line and all its stowaway fictions need
to be written in dark ink. So we deal in apertures,
we say, in the business of proportional reveal.
Twice, that I know of, it falls into place: once,
when sand in mortar is listening to rain
and again, when slate roof-tiles recall small words
in a ghost hand that rubbed them clean away.

On the Potential Uses of Detail

Cubes of colour borrowed from a bottle of underwater blue
(its two papery hydrangea braced for light), and a toy, white-
stockinged soldier in a case. On the painted mantelpiece,
the angle of the candlestick to the carriage clock is like
music on pause while someone (not me) steps out
of the room to change into last night's clothes.

The mirror is talking back to its pooled ghosts, reminding
them, I take it, that good luck is the absence of bad, much
of the time. My eyes, my tongue, are listening for a scheme
to reveal itself, a detail to prove the truth of it, a key
placed underneath the hearth by a hand in darkness too.

By which time, the varnish will be dry on another hour.
To the vermilion couch will fall the setting of the tone
so the composed room may give up on interpreting itself.
Through the window to the right, a way will be found
to paint ardour and rote as thin light on playing fields;

for the hedge to heed the barking dog, for a woman on a bike
to be made to think, I am of the world. This might as well be
where things settle, this where I am, this willing my heart
to keep time with the dark inside the drawer of the realistic
writing desk; with under the antique lid of the ring-box;
with every imaginable facet of the withheld story there.

The Yellow Vase

What say you to a window sill
in the Ceramics Hall, to angling it
between the minutes to either side
of the sun being certainly up?

To letting it tell no story but its own?
To give no label, so porcelain snatches
of sunlight and cloud be
its only inkling of real worlds?

Tapered onto its very mouth,
as though having only a single chance
to take from ballast
what needs matter most,

its emptiness, the certainty of this.
In the signal abeyance a body gifts
to the historical world, what is hoarded,
I ask you, and what offered, what released?

Grant this vase, between us both,
the shape of all desire. Have it stand
so light discloses every nerve
and membrane in its being.

Say the glaze must hold still;
the gold forget what it cannot contain
of blood or disappointment.
Say its open mouth must be

an antonym to every flower
kept from it all this while.
Say the space that you vacate,
I enter, wordlessly,

as if longing could be an end in itself,
the yellow fact of it being, finally,
something to open in sunlight,
something to hold against time.

Taking an Interest in the Decorative Arts

It spills over, what I write on paper, onto
counter tops and quilt covers, cushions,
tablecloths. Even the tulips lean into the whole
point of the vase, the wall clock rhymes

with the carriage clock, the nest of tables nests
between gold leaf and flock wallpaper.
The page is glazed with white tin glaze,
and every framing device brush-stroked

with the colour of its wall. No vase or teaspoon,
drape or lamp, distinguishes itself. The motif
is either artifice or else sincerity. You choose,
just as you might discern the sheen of water

from committed glass, the line of a mantelpiece
from the rim of a vase, the brink of that line
from a background pronounced by my hand,
my eye, my fastening design. The very dress

I choose to wear for you this day summers
a meaning of itself from every hall or landing
we walk through: blue words for sky or sea
and cornflower; yellow, for corn and heat.

Tonight, as every night, my house, my hours
will rid themselves of this enlivening art.
Colour and scheme will drain away, make
nothing of themselves, abstract still lifes.

We will wake to pristine detail, the white page
knowing what there is to know about being
in the world. As I push the door to whichever
room, I almost sense its every surface flinch.

Monet's Palette, Musée Marmottan

for Peter Fallon

The wood of the palette is
a notional pond, paint
suggesting petals, leaves,
blossom, even,

and the play of weather. The rim
of the palette is the edge
of the pond, his thumb arching
as the green bridge does

a clasp of shadow
by a willow tree
in the real world's
first impression.

In the dining room
with yellow walls
someone is saying one thing
and the garden says another.

But the room with no wall
is clear of words and facts
akin to names of paints
so colour makes one kind of sense

and texture makes another.
Between them, thumb and forefinger,
they draw the world on
to a skim of wood

as a pond held
in an outstretched palm

acquires depth and lustre,
rising to the light of day

to the moment when
paint applied to a palette
imagines itself a painting
and coheres.

Nothing goes to waste.
Sunset colour will do as well
for rainfall lacquering a summer pond
or cloud, perhaps, in a second draft,

midnight over rooftops,
an establishing city glow.
Faith. Finesse and carefulness.
Daylight edits its high hour,

learns to begin all over again,
only steadier this time,
if it's lucky: able to trust
the need for change,

the will to make good
on the promise, anew,
that one thought would
always call on the next,

one sensation pin a rhyme
onto another. It happens rightly
when it does, the way colour
and the shape of colour

come lightly through
so the canvas recalls the palette

as a stone in a Japanese garden does
mountains unknown to it.

And the paint remembers
the wooden palette as mist over
an inland field has something
of the ocean in it still,

the difference being one and the same
as oils make to grain and ridge,
everything worked out from there
in russet and violet; hidden and lit;

winter songs and summer songs,
the pond as stillness over time
from which is whittled a slip
of morning to ripen, even so.

The Hammershøi Sequence

THE INTERIORS OF VILHELM HAMMERSHØI

What is there? Windows
through windows, doors
that give onto other doors
as rooms of the future do,

and a woman, seated,
in whose neck light steadies
itself, silences the yellow
of streetlamps, so it begins,

the day. Errands and callers
unpick stillness from a frame
of hours in one hand,
silk thread in the other.

And she was there, held as a candle
set on a window sill is held
by the business of evening
flocked beyond the glass.

But that was years ago.
There were few enough callers
and the errands, such as they were,
were all too easily dispatched.

She spent her time believing one room
much the colour of another,
training herself to the truth
of a tabletop and a porcelain bowl

filled by her hand with cherries
and, once, with chanterelles.

The stove bellied with darkness
and the chair-back leaned into the wall.

A black dress empties and the room does too.
Her hands are no way strong enough
to lift from the floorboards
an idea of light

that she may know desire
or her body yield an intimate absence.
In the room of curtains that fall
to the floor, doors open as

unanswered questions through which
life and the opposite of life
pass into each other as sunlight
happening upon itself.

THE EXTERIORS OF VILHELM HAMMERSHØI

As if the half-night
when she hadn't kissed him
under the linden tree

had been abstracted
to the bricks and mortar
of a January day,

rooftops in the very shade
that had lined each promise
he'd made, and a sky

the colour of middle age;
every window an end in itself,
every front door ringing hollow.

THE COURTYARDS OF VILHELM HAMMERSHØI

Solitude being, as Montaigne said,
the calling back of the soul unto the self,

the lit window summons the dark
as if from one frame of mind to another,

as if from one future to a future opposite
runs a tripwire of desire.

THE SEASCAPES OF VILHELM HAMMERSHØI

The ship is a child's toy, unplayed with,
in a sea the colour of sky,

except for where light loosens the grey
as if darkness were a run of knots

to be solved, to be undone.
This sun could come as easily from her:

a yellow child that cannot sit still,
forever scattering dust motes or tossing high

the day. She would return it, gladly,
to her womb, this impulse;

feel on the open door of her body
its light, insistent fist.

THE LANDSCAPES OF VILHELM HAMMERSHØI

Between water reading itself a story
with no people in it

and fields, illegible, and a sky
that promises nothing,

least of all what will happen now,
are the trees

that do not believe in
any version of themselves

not even the one in which
they are apparently everyday trees

and not a sequence of wooden frames
for ordinary leaves.

THE INTERIORS OF VILHELM HAMMERSHØI

Her gone, the room would make no sense,
its silences turn sallow, its straight lines lag.
As it is, her collar infers the candle
and the window trim; also, the streetlamp

with its blatant street. She stows the future
in the folds of her skirt. The cells of the room
coalesce in the marrow of her bones
and her neck predicts a veritable world.

Who knows why a room turns itself inside
out to where a body cannot withstand
the sadness of chair-backs or linen cloths
or a teacup crammed with light?

Every room he will paint without her in it
will keep watch over her absence
as one would a sleeping child.
Every room with her in it too,

as though she could step into a life
of open doors and sunlit floorboards,
a gleam of voices, his hand on her skin,
being innocent of so much.

THE PORTRAITS OF VILHELM HAMMERSHØI

Specifically, the Double Portrait
of the Artist and his Wife, seen through a Mirror,

in which the light the width of her skirt,
and snatches of it on the wainscot and wall

but not for a second on his person,
standing where I stand, my life at his back,

in his black suit and his black frame,
acknowledges the gold of love

not being, maybe never being,
subdued by so definite dark.

Acknowledgements and Notes

Thanks are due to the editors of the following publications in which these poems, or versions of them, have appeared: *Boston Review, Causeway/Cabhsair, Clifden Anthology, The Dark Horse, Edinburgh Review, Irish Pages, The Irish Times, Irish University Review, Kaffeeklatsch, The Kenyon Review, Magma, The Manchester Review, The Moth, The North, Poetry Ireland Review, Poetry London, PN Review, Poetry Review, Poetry Salzburg Review, The Rialto, Southword, Stride, Sunday Miscellany* (RTÉ Radio), *Vallum* and *Yale Review*.

'The Landscapes of Vilhelm Hammershøi' was published in *The New Yorker*.

'The White Garden' and 'The Blue Garden' were set to music by Irene Buckley as part of *The Middle Kingdom* (a poetry, visual art and music collaboration on the theme of women's middle age) held at the Irish Arts Center in New York in February 2013. The event was supported by the University of Manchester.

'Monet's Palette, Musée Marmottan' appears in *Peter Fallon: Poet, Publisher, Editor and Translator,* edited by Richard Rankin Russell (Irish Academic Press, 2013).

'The Yellow Vase' was commissioned for *What We Found There* — an anthology of poems prompted by objects found in the National Museum of Ireland's collections (Dedalus Press, 2013).

Thanks are due to the Centre Culturel Irlandais in Paris for an artist residency in summer of 2010, during which several of these poems were written.

Thanks to John McAuliffe, Roger Rendell and Conor O'Callaghan for their suggestions and help. And special thanks, as ever, to Peter, Jean and the staff of The Gallery Press who make this possible and complete.